Poetry

FROM MY MIND TO YOURS

W. L. SAMUEL

authorHOUSE®

AuthorHouse™
1663 Liberty Drive
Bloomington, IN 47403
www.authorhouse.com
Phone: 1-800-839-8640

Published by AuthorHouse 12/10/2012

ISBN: 978-1-4772-9528-1
ISBN: 978-1-4772-9782-7

Library of Congress Control Number: 2012922993

Acknowledgements

To my wife, for her continual love and support,

To my parents, for simply being great

To my brother Skid, for all your support

Last but not least,

To Shihan G. Aschkar Jr. for giving me the warrior spirit to get up when knocked down and to endure by the principle of

"Beyond pain, there is no pain"

With love I thank you all.

Also by W. L. Samuel
Touching Widows
And coming soon: Coveting The First

Contents

Part 1 – Love

Marriage

We are one my love
dedicated to the perpetual flawlessness of our oneness
our uninterrupted flow of energy
brings us to a crest
and the intensity of our intimacy
brings out our best

We became one my love
when I entered your heaven
and caused your cloud to rain

We became one my love
when your joy became my joy
and your pain became my pain

We are one my love
even our hearts beat the same
flawless is our oneness
we share the same name.

My Essential

If only I could breathe the air
that was exhaled by you
if only I could be on the pillow
that you laid next to
then I would be face to face
embracing you

My nights are filled with fantasies of you
My sleep dominated by dreams of you

My body yearns to be near you
I can't exist I'm in need of you

If you were air, I would be breathing you.

A View Before Dying

Watching the miles of beauty
of the morning sky
Watching you the same way
before the flowers and the cries
freezing the precious moments
in every space in my mind
no room for sorrow
when approaching the time

Bliss must not be spoiled
by even a drop of tear
fading to the next realm
without a drop of fear
accepting the fate
that is assigned to me
because of the preciousness
you gave my mind to see.

For Your Love

It's not the receiving of
but the lack of
that caused my confusion
my pulsing heart
bleeds of pain
I need a transfusion
I have given so much of
and now I am in need of
who is there to dispense of
I am wanting of
I am needing of
I am of dying of
the lack of your love.

Amorometer

So many have tried
To measure the immeasurable
some have compared love to the ocean's depth
but to lose that love would be to surface
and to surface and not decompress leads to death
history reveals to us Jesus
because of love he died for us all
since then men have become martyrs
for women who had them enthralled
the depth of love will make one forgive
that same love will make one kill
but all the measurements leads to one conclusion
that love is infinite
and infinite still

Love

The unmistakable knowledge
of the intangible power can leave one powerless,
for when it is felt, one is compelled
to react based on its degree
for fear of the loss of it,
one will do the unthinkable to preserve it
and for those who are without it
live miserably

True Joy

There is true joy
in watching a son grow
You are only five
and it's amazing all the things you already know

Even a second language
you were able to grasp
and in the pool all by yourself
you were doing laps

I feel so proud
as I watch you practice tennis
and because I am there
you swing extra hard trying not to miss
but if you did
that would be ok
you'll get hugs
and kisses anyway

To me
You'll always be daddy's boy
son
You bring me the world of joy.

Cause of Death

He bellowed when he saw her give her love to another
Instantly the death of love
made him the beneficiary of grief
he cried a cry so deep
his soul escaped him, never to return.

Love Burns

A lover of pain some say I am
accepting abuse again and again

this mental torture unearths the desire
to take vengeance on my princess of fire

She keeps burning me and burning me
Then comes with an apology

My princess, sorry doesn't numb the pain
Especially when you're hurting me again and again

Though, with these burns I choose to live
because when you love someone
you continue to forgive

Home

Listen
the gentle breeze brings the
melody of his voice to my ears
I knew he was coming home
Inhale
The strength of his fragrance
which captivates me year after year
I knew he was coming home
Look
Into his happy eyes as they float in rivers of joy
when he came home to me
Kiss
with passion that bonds
two souls alloy
when he came home to me

My Love

He was a one man army
He went on a mission
To save his country
Behind enemy lines he took the risk
now by his country
he's greatly missed
some believe he is dead
but she knows he is alive
he is a P.O.W.
trying to survive
he only hopes she helps him to be free
because the risk wasn't for him
but for the love of his country.

Not Enough

A bouquet of purple roses
Just a prelude for my kiss
Love permeates my mind
As the early morning mist
Each day when I thank God
I include you in my prayer
life would be empty without you
For no one else compares

Lacking nothing attached to passion
for all my love I give
touching you ever so softly
Because you are sensitive
Each day I must say "I love you"
To display it is never too much
My love is too great to express in one day
So Valentine's just isn't enough

Total Meaning

How do I know that I love you?
because no hour is complete without you in it
It matters not how involved I am in my work
Images of you pervade my mind
with your smile and your eyes
with their many expressions

How do I know that I love you?
because your flaws become
imperceptible to me
all I see is perfection

How do I know that I love you?
because when I rise in the mornings
I want the air that I breathe
to be scented with your fragrance

How do I know that I love you?
because I class you with the angles
below God, but above man

Finally my beloved
I know that I love you because
If I was a word
you would be my prefix and my suffix
giving me total meaning
I would be incomplete without you.

Our Road Map

The year was ninety-four
October, day eight
I made vows to my queen
To fulfill our fate

Eighteen years have passed
and sometimes things went wrong
but we pulled out our map
found our course and stayed strong

It takes love and commitment
it takes God and faith
it takes compromise and understanding
to keep one's soul-mate

So when we drive down
relationship's bumpy road
we ask God
to lighten our load

And if by chance
one of us do snap
we pull out our bible
because it's our road map

The Crush

As always, he sat in silence while he waited
every few seconds his eyes shifted to the door

as she stepped in, his heart palpitated
the pre-arranged encounter felt better than before
he inhaled deeply as she passed him
in an attempt to take in the essence of her scent
his mind recording details
remaining cognizance

his eyes watched her fingers
as they manipulated the chalk
and when she turned from the blackboard
he watched her lips when she talked
with her tongue between her teeth
she produced the word 'the'
he watched her in slow-motion
he was captivated by her
she has inner beauty
and it was shining out
it made him wished to be a word
so he too could be in her mouth

Oh yes, secretly he wanted her
as she stood before the class
his imagination became graphic
it mentally caressed her ass

Suddenly he halted
his day-dream took him pass noon
saying 'damn' to himself once again
for the session ended too soon

Body Heat

Nights without you are painful for me
I need to feel the warmth of you next to me
the scent of your hair, indelible in my nose
from the shampoo you used, fragrance of rose
when your pores open
your essence I get
in your arms I am wrapped
bathed in your sweat

Nights without you, my epitomes of fear
so brush me with your fingertips
let me know you're still there

Nights without you, leaves my bed cold
whisper to me darling
that you're still there to hold

Nights without you, have come to an end
because we both took an oath
never to separate again.

Visions

When I look into your eyes
I see all your thoughts of me
I see the things you fear of me
I see the things you desire of me
And I see your undying love for me

When I look at you
I see an intelligent and beautiful woman
A woman so strong
But yet so fragile
I see a woman I want to love and protect
For all the days of my life

When I look at you
I just want to hold you
And to have that moment in time suspended

When I look at you
I see many things
Things I never saw before
I see visions of life,
visions of you
of you being my wife.

Relationship

A seed it is just a little seed

But with patience

Constant caring

Constant loving

The gardeners made the seed a huge tree

Life

To breathe is to know of your own existence
To laugh is to experience the happiness in it
Hatred is the emptiness within one's self
And love in all it's beauty
is the understanding of life

The Ultimate Power

Everyone wants it
not everyone receives it
when given, some simply accept it
most thrive off it
others reject it
and some fear it
fear of the unknown
fear of no control
love, you can't control it
it controls you.

You Remind Me

What is it about your face?
It reminds me of the rising sun
The dawns tranquility

What is it about your eyes?
They remind me
of the tiger's fury and the dove's serenity

What is it about your lips?
They remind me of
An irresistible iridescent pink, pure beauty

What is it about your breast
They remind me of a man's most sweetest fruit
And a baby's most natural pillow

What is it about your hands
They remind me of a gentle stream
flowing down a mountain
the magical touch of sensuality

What is it about you
You remind me of love
and the glory it brings in life.

To Know Is To Be

I've seen your face, so I know what beauty is
I've touched your body, so I know what lust is
I've been apart from you, so I know what pain is
I've heard your cries, so I know what sadness is
I've felt your joy, so I know what happiness is
I will die for you, so I know what love is.

Destiny

What vision is this I see?
Of love, of beauty, could it be?
Is it possible for life to be so kind?
For this vision I've searched and now I find
Perhaps my desires are causing hallucinations
But logic reveals reality not imagination
And who must I thank for this unity
For this vision of love, of beauty, is destiny.

Spellbound

I am so in love and I can't help this feeling
What spell did you cast, to make me so revealing?
Locked in my mind are thoughts of you
And out from my mouth the words
I love you
If you take a close look
You will see the sparkle in my eyes
I'm made of steal, but for you I'll cry

Never doubt my love
For I'm a fish on you line
But I hope I have you hooked
And you're also mine

For I'm still perplexed
By the magic spell you've cast
But I pray to God
Forever it will last.

Feeling Love

So many words have been used to describe that feeling
That sensation of bliss when we first kissed
And all the kisses that followed after

You know that feeling
That's the feeling we both felt
at the very same moment in time
when our bodies transcends arousal
uniting our souls and minds

You know that feeling
That's the feeling you feel
when you wake in the morning
and your eyes search for the face
of the one who gives you that feeling

That's the feeling that has my mind
like the morning's fog
I cannot see the word to describe the feeling
but you know that feeling.

Fill Me

My eyes need to be filled with the details of your face
I don't even have to touch you
as long as we share the same space
may it be laying, sitting or standing
as long as your aura is felt
just being in your presence
Is enough for my heart to melt
and if by chance I cannot see you
then let your perfume fill my nose
at least I could imagine
that you are somewhere close.

True Expression

I am not attempting to plagiarize
As I write my next line
But darling you are so beautiful to me
Beautiful because you are my life

You are the reason my heart beats
I feel you in my veins instead of blood
I live because of you
There's no exaggeration in my expression
No man on earth has a deeper love
than the love I have for you

When I went astray
you were the angle that brought me back to Jesus
I love you
And without you in my veins
There is no life for me.

Dovetail

It's mystically divine
how we came together
a perfect fit
we were made for each other
but there is no relationship
void of turbulence
when it came
we cuddled close
so it came and went
our love has a flair of divinity
it's constant in it's forward motion
building strength by the minute
no question of our devotion
content we are
deep in our love
yet some say someday love will fail
but jealous thinking
will never separate
the bond of our dovetail.

Nurtured

The lucky flower I am
Picked and given to you
Death did not become me
For in your hands
I grew.

Like The First

The anticipation of a desired kiss leaves me breathless
Fixed eyes frozen on your lips
Hostages to their beauty
I am in love, helplessly in love
Each kiss feeling like the first
With that special tingle
The tingle I long for
The tingle I hope for
I am breathless for the tingle that I thirst.

Rapture

I am trapped in your rapture
But I have no desire to escape
Spellbound by your movements
You body and it's shape
When you touch me I am dazzled
Not confused, but amazed
When you kiss me it's magic
Defying gravity, I raise
I am trapped in your rapture
A world of euphoria
Everything so perfect
I will never leave here
Every nerve connected
When you take me in
When I'm in your rapture
It feels like heaven within.

Part 2 – Spiritual

Transformation

I'm not who I thought I was
I am different now, different somehow
Remolded-refashioned-reformed
My transition seen, but not conceived
By the natural mind which still will not believe

I'm not who I used to be
I am different now, and I know why and how
I found Jesus and He transformed me
catapulting my mind to the mystical realm
where all things become a possibility

I understand the true definition of power now
beyond it's physical meaning
Look into my eyes and see the light within me gleaming
I'm not who I use to be
Today I live for Jesus
Because his spirit lives in me.

Cold World

Cold cold cold were the icicled eyes
Piercing his flesh with their stare
Bitter bitter bitter were the passerby words
Yet he feigned he did not care

Hidden underneath was a crying being
Carrying the burden of sin
Wishing it could be washed away from him
Like the exfoliation of dead skin

In the church he sought refuge
Thought for sure he would find a friend
But in the pew all around him
Their smiles were just pretend

Handshakes and hugs
A big hoax how they lived
With lips that preached love
And hearts that don't forgive

Cold cold cold,
but thank God for his grace
In this cold cold world
He doesn't need them to see God's face.

Live

It's not enough to simply live life
I feel responsible to give life, to feed life
To water existing seeds
Helping flowers grow from dying weeds
My purpose is to transform autumnal modes
to vibrant springs
and withering trees to blossoming things

It's is not enough to simple live
I speak of the eternal life He wants to give
From the shadows in the forest
Where all secrets are hid
But you deceive yourselves
For believing He doesn't know what you did
Repent and let me feed you with the word
Like the honey bee and humming bird
From a flower in bloom
Eat and live life before your last day spells doom.

The Imp

Every now and again
I'm attacked by it
It makes suggestions in my ear
While on my shoulder it sits

Evil thoughts will then
Slowly creep into my mind
Dividing my personality
One for good and one for crime

It said obtain pleasure, obtain wealth
Anything desired, it will help get
But a voice came from deeper within
Saying, follow it and be filled with regrets

Constant is the battle
between the two of me
This week triumphs good
but next week we'll have to see

And to the reader of this poem
Every word is true
Beware of the imp
Because on your shoulder it sits too.

Forgiveness

Oh Lord my heart is engulfed in sorrow
You know the many nights
Which I have cried into the morrow

Leaving my eyes the color of blood
And my pillows once dry
Were the aftermath of a flood

Oh Lord you know the reason for my despair
I became a Judas
to a friend so dear
Now I want back that guarded trust
Which I lost in an insane state
of financial lust

Oh Lord I have already received it from you
But forgiveness from a friend
I need that too
Please help me Lord with this quest
Because the guilt I feel
will not let me rest

Oh Lord grant me a reunion of face to face
To be like old friends
And once again embrace.

Vessel

There once was a time I was lost
Exiled from life, Exiled from the cross

My body, just a vessel which they used
I traveled with seven, which kept me bemused

When they were in, I never stood still
I was driven to sin, till each one had its fill

Without question, I obeyed their commands
Wanting to resist, but could never take a stand
Until one day when I uttered His name
I felt a change, and knew that He came
Inside of me the light came on
The demons packed and are now all gone

They used to laugh and say "can't get rid of us"
That's because they didn't know,
I had a friend name Jesus

The Plague

As mortals we are born plagued with an infirmity
No injection can cure
This curse of infamy
Heaven and hell
are as real as you and me
this we all know
but still choose iniquity
that's how sick sin have us
to prefer death through eternity
than eternal life,
a life lived in morality
it's believed a few may find a cure
if in their hearts there is purity
but the plague of sin have the rest of us
so hells gate is surety

Spreading Faith

Allow me to share with you
the secret of the parable
you don't have to be a scholar
to grasp what is credible

For hundreds of years
This mystery lies before their eyes
But with science
They compromise

Misleading the people
With thoughts scientific
to discredit the truth and power
of a God that's mystic

Allow me to share with you
What is hidden, but is not
The revelation of God's power
Depends on the faith you've got

Exorcism

Bear witness
As I slaughter demons with my ink
What I write they will read
Read again, then rethink
The clock ticks
Jesus is coming soon
Pay attention to the signs
Famine, diseases, wars and typhoons
"Lord remember me"
many people will wail
make your change now
before the ship of repentance sail
God is Love
And you will be forgiven
But first you must confess
All that is hidden
Now if you're still not convinced
Of these words from my pen
The demon is still in you
So read them again.

My Oasis

My journey across the desert
Was taken all alone
My canteen was empty
And my mind almost gone

I had images of my soul mate
Of how she abandoned me
And I laid there in the sand
Hoping a dune will cover me

As the night's sky showed its beauty
Jesus crossed my mind
He would want me to survive this
So we can meet again in time

With my body dehydrated
And the desert having nothing to give
Jesus became my Oasis
Just so I can live

Holy Firmament

Kneeling under the canopy of blue sky
This firmament become my tabernacle
My tongue sing praises to the most high
For His mercies and His miracles

Out in the open I express my glee
Even before those who opposes me

With impediments
In my path to Zion
But can't be brocaded
I'm still moving on

My tabernacle is the canapé of blue sky
Every where I go
I give praises to the Most High

Spiritual is the battle for the soul
With a strong will stay adamant
Praying as I do daily
With my eyes to the firmament

Part 3 – Assorted

Lone Dove

When will the war end?
When will peace begin?
Why can't my voice be heard?
When I scream peace on earth
I feel like a lone dove
In a sky filled with no love
I'm sick of seeing torture
By the bald eagle and the desert vulture
Why can't they see what I see?
A macabre aftermath it will be
Industry profits just an illusion
To the greedy minds in total confusion
Failing to understand the true cost
The thousands upon thousands
of lives that have been lost
when will the war end?
When will peace begin?
Well maybe, just maybe
Not till the world ends.

Regrets

Tearless cries in the night
An open mouth with no screams
I'm exhausted from suppressing
The emotions not seen

Still cannot sleep
Though tormented and fatigued
Perhaps it would be best
To join the necropolis league

My cries for help silenced
By my own pretence of strength
But alone when I'm alone
that same pretense went

I considered the truth
When my weakness emerged
That my body and earth
Should soon become merged

After all, its my fault
For the help I did not get
But in life, we live
And we die with regrets.

Father to Son

Whatever you do my son
Remember the days of fun
Remember the nights when I tucked you in
Reading to you, tickling you
To see that ear-to-ear grin

Whatever you do my son
Take comfort in knowing
That as you grow
My love for you keeps growing

Whatever you do my son
Extract the good from me
And beware of the slander
The negative names of me

I've been called an adulterer
Crooked-embezzler, a thief
I've been called an extortioner
And even the maker of grief

It is said my son
That every rose has its thorns
But only let the good part of me
Through you, live on.

The Blank

The keys of the keyboard clattered
As the words were put on the page
realizing the story was about him
He became filled with rage

Fifty words per minute
between each word a space
he was on every line, in every verse
but neither upper or lower case

Throughout the story
You never notice him
Because on the page he held no rank
Like many are treated in society's page
He was the nothing, the misfit
The blank

Survivor

Many thought I was down for the count
It's what's expected when one crash and burn
Don't be a pessimist when one falls down
It's life's cycle and you too may have a turn

I live to regret my symbolic death
When all feelings died in their eyes
But not accepting what they thought of me
I held my head up and prepared to rise

With calculated steps I found my niche
Honing and cultivating it
Gradually but surely I did persevere
Until I came out of the pit

Experience is the greatest educator
I live, I have fallen, I have learned
And today I have risen from the ashes
Because I stayed positive when I crashed and burned

The choice is yours if you're one who have failed
Is to reject or accept the norm said
It's not your situation, but your state of mind
You can choose to survive or you can stay dead

Autopsy

The cause of death – inconclusive
was the autopsy's report
but I know it was poverty
with what the cost of living extort

From medical expenses
to food price and gas hike
are the reasons why we die
not eat, walk or bike

Too frequent are the cases
I see hypertension on the increase
Mental stress overload
Is synonymous to decease

I am not trying to be judgmental
my sins I cannot hide
but just to get their daily bread
I've seen morals cast aside

What would you do? if the bank was taking your home
What would you do? if you were losing all that you own

The autopsy is a lie
because even I can clearly see
from the state of the economy
he died from poverty

Riches To Rags

Have you ever been up?

Then suddenly fell down
Your whole world turned upside down

Rapid unexpectedness of debt increase
Joining the sea of the financially deceased

Every attempt to move forward
Feels like you're in reverse
Depression takes its toll
And life feels like a curse

Wanting to end it,
But that's the cowards way out
So you keep on the gloves
But still losing the bout

Medication can't seem to help you sleep
Thoughts of poverty sinking in deep

Sane or insane how did you get so low?
The recession left you with no where to go

From riches to rags, oh what a twist
Who would've thought that your life, my life,
Would turn out like this

Looking Glass

When he looked in the mirror
he was a stranger to himself
unfulfilled and the opposite
of the cobwebbed dreams on the shelf

Looking back at him
were a combatant set of eyes
mental swords drawn
and kamikaze battle cries

From the free-falling clone
who jumped without his chute
realizing he was nothing
but a losing substitute

Of the man he wanted to be
but couldn't make the grade
concluding to himself
winners are born and not made

Breaking the mirror
so he would not have to see
the man in the mirror
was looking directly at me

Too Dark

From fresh air to stink air
How can I cope?
Many times I contemplated on using the rope
And other times I envisioned
Slitting my wrist or my throat
Why?
Because I can't breathe anymore
Inside I'm suffocating
Desperate for fresh air
I feel my heart palpitating
And now
With tear filled eyes
I holler for them to hear me
Fist bruised and swollen
Pounding padded walls for them to free me
Claustrophobia
Joined the list of enemies
Hyperventilating
Because of an attack from anxiety
The stench in the air
My lungs refuse to keep
Dear God give me fresh air
Or let me go to sleep

Addicted

I can't remember when
But I was still young then
When I first kissed her
She made my vision blur
Her name is Nicotine
She didn't smell so clean
But that was all right with me
I love how she made me feel
One day I met her older sister
A chick name Ganjacita
I kissed her the same way
She blew my mind all day
When Nicotine caught us
I said "baby don't fuss"
Your sister is my new friend
The two of you will make a great blend
That started a relationship
I couldn't keep them from my lips
And if I let a week pass
I would be a miserable ass
because they're my beauty queens
my Ganjacita and my Nicotine

Earth

I shake, I cry, I even erupt
I warned them of the danger
But they just would not stop
They destroyed what I produced
Converting what's natural
to be misused and abused
why can't they see
I can only take care of them
If they take care of me
My seas they drill
My trees they kill
If they don't stop, soon them I will
Their machines, a constant threat
My canopy fearing death
Their time will come for regret
For these people seem to forget
That my death brings their death

Hidden

Compassion if true
Will have its own well
Even if hidden at times
Its owner can tell

Some choose to express
Their emotions to all
While others conceal
Erecting a wall

As for me, I'm private
And have been for years
Alone at my well
I've pulled buckets of tears

I hurt twice as much
At least that's what I believe
Than those who lose face
Those who openly grieve

Nevertheless, I give ode to condolences
It's no offence to show pain
I give ode to the barricades
Tears are tears all the same

On The Brink

I've watched seemingly sane men
Do a hundred and eighty degrees mental turn
A drastic increase in stress
Can easily cause the mind to burn

Sometimes I am made to wonder
If my own mind has flipped
Because on the brink of depression
I myself have tipped

Like a plane with engine failure
I was losing altitude
And only those who were dearest
Noticed the changes in my mood

With all the love from my family
I still felt so alone
Inside me filled with turbulence
But on my face a smile was shown

Now my hope is to glide
On a meadow I can manage
Landing safely from my troubles
Without sustaining damage

Like those I have seen before
Who've had a mental turn
They never leveled off
But crashed landed and burned

Possessed

What comes over me
Like snow flakes on pine trees
A winter forecast that is inevitable
But this season comes to me frequently
It's an obsession that plagues me
My refuge is temporary
Somehow, someway
In the midnight it finds me
I'm sick of myself
Being possessed by lust
Sleeping pills never aiding
I wake, for the orgasm rush is a must
Eager to be engulfed
To find solace between two thighs
But if that's not available
Then my hand would be suffice
Dawn brings a new season
In the sunlight I find peace
At dusk the winter trespasses
Waking the lecher to feast

Ex Soldier

Their war has ended, but the feud just begun
In my head, the screams still echoes on
Uniform closeted, in civilian I'm clad
But not a day passes by, when I don't see Bagdad
My discharge honorable, a hero not disgraced
But hidden in my files, I'm now a mental case
Physically fit they say, in fact even superb
But no longer reliable, for my mind is disturbed
Because every so often, I would fold to a cocoon
Reaction from flashes, of how they died in my platoon
Sometimes I feel I am the dead soldier left behind
For I am alone in my struggle, this war in my mind
There is no relief from my comrades' dying shouts
So to silence my own, I put the nozzle in my mouth
For some reason I could not find the courage to do it
Perhaps I'm still sane, if not, tomorrow I'll pull it.

Economic Downturn

Is it possible to love my country
but dislike my government
is it their fault that many are displaced
can't meet the mortgage or the rent
unemployment still skyrocketing
and their answer is the new term
trying to pacify us by saying
global economic down-turn
I'm sick of those words
It's a problem void of solutions
Affecting only the poor and the middle class
The rich care less about resolutions
Presidents and prime ministers
Conspire to use the term
A subliminal acceptance of poverty
Global Economic Down-Turn

The Musician In Me

I am not a musician
But often I dream
To touch the strings of the guitar
To make my fans scream
Feeling the vibrations
From every chord that I play
As my fingertips dance
On the guitar's highway
From the rhythm of rock
To the rhythm of blues
It doesn't matter
Which music I choose
As long as I can hold
A guitar in my hand
To touch the strings
For all of my fans

Midnight Cry

The midnight bleeds for mercy
Silently a child cries out
Sinfully touched by her father
As she was ordered not to shout
Age six the mind so fragile
A time to nurture and groom
Instead, she was shattered
and put on a path of doom
when she confided in her mother
she made no effort to inspect
if this is not a lack of love
then it was a sure sign of neglect
in her teens she was stronger
so her father left her alone
but the molestation did its damage
for the child in her was gone
her emotions roam aimless
in want of the right of way
and from time to time she wants to die
because her father made her gay

Untimely

Compare me to the flower
which received no sun
next to a stream of water
but roots received none

I am he underneath
With bloodless veins
Long past the stage
of aches and pains

it came too swift
to remember how or why
it came too swift
I was not ready to die

Dead Words

My behavior
A direct result of your tongue being a stranger to the truth
Meaningless words reaching my ears gates
But never passing through
Actions become the only proof
Speak not
Unless your words collaborate with movements
The defect of your character
Drastic is the need for improvement
Unvarnished
Is how I come to you
Reciprocate
Don't be a stranger to the truth

The Need

In the head sounded
The bells of economic emergency
A paranoid mind in search
For a solution to the urgency
Thoughts of his family becoming destitute
Erupted in his brain
Creeping hunger only intensified the pain
The fittest survive in no-mans land
And the need to survive brings out the beast in a man
Moral values become a thing of the past
First things first, cure the hunger fast
But later in the calm sits a quiet remorse
For the steps that were taken, was not the right course
Let us not condemn him, lets try to forgive
For someone we know may release their beast to live.

Ashes

He was my best friend
And he asked me to follow him
To an estate where he once lived
When his eyes become dim
In my hands I held him
Before releasing him to the atmosphere
A cloud of him filled the air
Settling amongst the grass
Manipulated by the wind for the last.

I Transmit

I am an artist doing what an artist do
Like the painter or the musician
I too transmit to you
Feelings
Feeling emerge from my pen
To you the audience
Who loves to be on the receiving end
Of an artist exposed emotions
Touching you in its plain
Or a form that's sometimes abstract.
You empathize then retain
The feelings
That you could not admit
But I, the artist, the poet
My feelings I transmit.

The Cry

Today was a day different
From any other day in my life
In my father's eyes I have betrayed him
And those were the words that came from his mouth
Like arrows through my heart
The betrayal was my failure
I have failed one time too many
Today was a day different from any other day in my life
For the first time I saw my father struggle
struggle to hold back tears
so I spared him, I let him hold on to his strength
and I – I cried for him

Inspiration

I am nothing being everything
I am everything being nothing
I am ink transformed to words
Words completing the thoughts
Of the holder of the pen
Who is nothing, but becomes everything
Everything when inspired by true love
Which causes me – the ink
to flow to the end of the masterpiece of words
words after put together
is called
poetry

Great Men

Great men of time have been imprisoned
For humanity or other political reasons
It's my turn to contribute to this trend
For we live in a world of perfidious men
And when I am free
I'll be pardoned for the crime
When I am free
I too will be one of the great men of times

Father's Nightmare

A late night scream wakes him
Again his bed sheets wet from his sweat
His little boy's voice calls him
Daddy I can't reach you yet
An out-stretched hand faced him
But faded when trying to reach back
The illusions not stopping
The mental hurricane causing him to crack
Like the hour-glass
That he threw against the wall
In an attempt to stop the time
So his pain can take a fall
But it still stands
And suffocates him each time he closes his eyes
For the son he couldn't hold
When "Daddy" he cries

The Lodge

The release of truth
Is a policy ascribed to the youth
As for men, they must lie
Or be convicted and condemned
By the same policy they supplied
To the nation that they fooled
Brain washed since nursery school
Deception is the creed
Of the players involved
Even the election is a hoax
For the president to revolve
The eyes will see
Only the picture they paint
But true evil exist
Under the guise of a saint
A world within a world
Of the secret society I speak
Enforcing their policies
To the blind and the meek

Impact

The truth behind the war
Could only be told
By the crying out
Of dead soldiers souls
Read the headlines
From the press release
Day after day
Body counts increase
The families and friends
Know now what the chief already knew
But it was the soldiers not him
That felt the bombs when they blew
And those families and friends
They too felt the blast
Trying to hold on to memories
Of dead soldiers past.

Missing Him

In the coldness of winter
He left his hand-prints on the pane
Looking though the window
Wishing for his dad again
He didn't see him coming
So to his bed he ran
Throwing his pillow in frustration
As the tears began
His mother walked in to comfort him
Then she too started to weep
Because she didn't know how to tell him
That his father, the Marine was asleep.

Still Primitive

I was born into this uncivilized world
That claims civility
Take a closer look
And see the truth that I see
Unscrupulous politicians
With their counterfeit integrity
Secretly filling their pockets
While innocent people die
From their guns and rockets
With my own eyes
I've witnessed senseless executions
Yet they claim to be civilized
They are no better than the priest
Who openly praised God
And behind closed doors sodomize
Open your eyes and see how they live
They speak civility
But live primitive

In Need Of An Ear

This morning I said I would not write anything
I did not want to convey my state of melancholy
But with my pen in hand, I guess I'm impulsive
I hope it's not my folly
Cheer up, cheer up,
I scream in my head
But the voice only ricochet
before it went dead
I would not cry
I would rise above this woe
Oh no, too late
The rivers in my eyes began to overflow.
I said I wouldn't write this morning
I didn't want to share my melancholy
I said I wouldn't write this morning
But I needed to talk to somebody.

Loneliness

Must be a man with a heart of stone
In my mind where I stand alone
Away from you, so far from home
In a different world is where I roam
A million miles, a million miles

Heavenly Father please stop the pain
How much longer before I go insane
I wish I can get high off the ground
Where my feet can't touch till they cut me down
A million miles, a million miles

What can you see when your eyes are closed?
What can you feel when you're comatose?
Darkness is what you see
Emptiness is what you feel
Heavenly Father I can't stand the pain
It won't be long before I go insane
A million miles, a million miles

Eternity

He dreamed to be free,
For so long he dreamed of freedom
Freedom of pain, freedom of sadness
And finally he took his dream to another level
He dreamt of the freedom of all things.
The ultimate freedom, to be eternally free
He dreamt of his death.

Lost In The Realm

How terrible the tricks one's mind plays
Causing one to scream from hallucinating disasters
Wishing to die as the mind race faster
Taking you in and out of dimensions
Being trapped in time, losing all sense of direction
Believing to be a patient
Induced with lethal injection
Or being a beast paranoid by rejection
And scratching the hands when there is no irritation
But believing the ants are causing that sensation
Oh how terrible the tricks one's mind plays
At any given time nights or days.

The Earth

It lives, it breathes, it gives us what we need
So we can breathe
We destroy it, but why,
Because we're fools with greed
For profits in industries
We take it away
Without the realization
Of the price we pay.

Death

It's calling me and calling me, but I refuse to go
It's not my time, I'm not ready for the trip below
I can feel it behind me as it creeps
It wants to make me a victim of its eternal sleep
I walk around frantically, not knowing what to do
Because in my head I hear it saying,
"I'm coming to get you"
I love my life, I refuse to die, but death persist
The six feet deep, the eternal sleep
I can't resist.

Infancy

The age of innocence
so young so carefree
Always experimenting
because they're filled with curiosity
They whimper at times
simply to get their way
and as soon as that's accomplished
again they start to play
some are quick to shed tears
when they think they did bad
but that's simply another method
to trick their mom and dad
for when we look at the faces of innocence
their wisdom we fail to see
for they're far more intelligent
than what they appear to be
now we must cherish the days
of those adorable entities
for the age of innocence
will soon be memories

Tears Within

He carries a smile on his face, but inside he cries
He awaits the moments, the day that he dies
He doesn't want to cause his family pain, but life is rotten
He'll soon be a memory, then he'll soon be forgotten
No one understands the only freedom is death
But he does, and prays for the moment he takes his last breath
He can't stand the pain he is going through
The feeling of helplessness, not knowing what to do
His brain explodes over and over again
Because of the hell he is living in
And no one knows he wishes to die
Because he carries a smile on his face,
But inside he cries.

The Rising Sun

Look and observe the elegance of dawn
The sky so magnificent with its crimson hue
Then little by little
Puffy white clouds and a touch of blue
Revealing an iridescent yellow
The rays burst through
And clouds forming pictures
Giving an extravagant view
And out of the darkness
This scene came
So enjoy it while it lasts
For no two are the same.

Liberation

It's happening right before my eyes
Tormented men with horrifying cries
Trapped in a society with no equality
Being abused by authority and stripped of dignity
Exercising the thought that they must rebel
To initiate the war some felt compelled
It's death or freedom, this, many contemplated
Wanting to die, being men liberated.

New Generation

Babies being abandoned by fathers who aren't good
Young ladies having babies who aren't fit for motherhood.

These are signs of the era when men self-destruct
Failing to follow the path that our elders constructed

Promiscuous is the behavior that some may choose
Becoming victims of the plague, then their lives they lose

While committing adultery they constantly press their luck
But these are the times when men self-destruct

Babies being born to parents who neglect
and children growing up giving parents no respect

But all this happen when men reject instructions
for this is the time for man's self-destruction.

A Bed Of Roses

Hot summer day, but he could not feel a thing
Nor hear the children's laughter or the bells that ring

For he dreamed within a dream and saw darkness as it came
Envisioning himself at peace within a wooden frame

A headboard made of marble extended from the deep
Never awaking from the horror, for under a bed of roses he sleeps.

Parental Care

One responsible for the existence of another
Receives the title father or mother
With this title comes the responsibility
Of protecting the young from life's treachery
For under the wings, children have no fear
They experience the love and parental care

Guardians too must do their part
And protect their children with all their hearts
Any other way is unthinkable
for a child may be scarred and for life be miserable
so mothers and fathers please give ear
and show your child parental care.

Tree's Last Words

Leave me I've fallen, the greedy has smitten me
Children can no longer play with me
Birds can no longer sing to me
For profits my life is brought to an end
The ozone destroyed, what then?
They rid of me who gives oxygen
Farewell-farewell
For profits my life is brought to an end
Farewell-farewell

Premonitions of Macabre

Twisting and turning from hagridden thoughts
Running and running, but continuously caught

By malignant creatures who moves stealth in the night
I'm losing control now, overwhelmed in fright

Can't stand the horror, so I scream and scream
Awaken myself from the terrifying dreams

Of death and decay happening whenever I sleep
I think that's the time the villains creep

Staying hidden in the closets and under my bed
Until I fall asleep, then they enter my head.

Oklahoma

Children's laughter turning into screams
Another holocaust was what it seems

Bloodshed and tears
Another tragedy appears

The innocent suffers from the politically insane
Who tried to prove a point, but the only thing gained

Was torment and sorrow from a madman's plot
Now condemned to hell and in jail shall rot

There must be a better way to deal with problems
By taking innocent lives will never solve them.

Just Like You

Teach me daddy, lead me to the portal of knowledge
So I can enter the realm of understanding
Gaining wisdom with every step behind you
Because I want to be just like you dad,
I want to be just like you
I admire the way you groom me
With a polite voice and gentle hands
And if I slip you scold me, with care so I'll understand
Your shoes are had to fill dad
But someday I promise I will dad
Because I want to be just like you dad
I want to be just like you

Life

Mother Earth, Mother Earth
Tree blossom, child's birth
It's all the same, all good
Could be flesh, could be wood
Keep them safe
Keep them alive
We need each other, in order to survive.

Move On

Is it for love or the fear of him
Is it for shelter or no self-esteem
Is it self hate or masochism
Why does she stay and kill her dream?

No silent nights for the sleep deprived
Neighbors rise as she laments
The police were called, but were sent away
her bleeding lips deemed an accident

The same excuse
was given last week
for the two black eyes
and swollen cheeks

The time before that
she had her meals through straws
she claimed it was dental work
must be a new name for broken jaw

She died before dying
lived for him to the end
Don't stay and kill your dreams
Move on my battered friends

Who Am I

Each page I write I fall deeper in the spell
Becoming characters in the stories I tell

Even when I read other authors books
Their personalities I also took

Some days I am a doctor, some days a cook
Some days a hero-cop, other days a crook

I even played rolls of the critically insane
Only to discover I truly felt their pain

A master of my mind I was thought to be
But which one is the real me of me

I pretend so much I seem to lose track
Now it's so hard to find me back

Paragraph after paragraph, page after page
Became my reality, my world a stage

And if I could do it all over again
I would still live my life inside my pen

No regrets when it's time to die
Even if I'm still asking, who am I?

About the Author

In his novel 'Touching Widows', W. L. Samuel promised to tell more of himself. He lives on the beautiful island of Antigua. He enjoys swimming, tennis and hiking. He gets most of his inspiration while sitting under a tree at the beach. The cool breeze magnifies his meditation.

He promises to tell more in his next book 'Coveting The First'.